SPIRITUAL ME

A PRACTICAL SPIRITUAL GUIDE FOR THE TIMES WE LIVE IN

JO BROTHERS

Spiritual Me - A Practical Spiritual Guide For The Times We Live In

www.spiritualme101.com

First Printing, 2015

Copyright © 2015 Jo Brothers

ISBN 978-0-9941093-2-3

All rights reserved.

This book or any portion thereof may not be reproduced or used in any manner whatsoever without the express written permission of the publisher except for the use of brief quotations in a book review.

Disclaimer

This book is not intended as a substitute for the medical advice of physicians. The reader should regularly consult a physician in matters relating to his/her health, and particularly with respect to any symptoms that may require diagnosis or medical attention.

Published by:
Perpetuity Media
PO Box 4444
Shortland Street
Auckland 1140
New Zealand

www.perpetuitymedia.com

Published in New Zealand
Printed in the United States of America

About the Author

Hi, my name is Jo, thank you for taking the time to read this book. Some background on me, I am naturally intuitive and grew up in a loving family environment that encouraged me to incorporate my intuition into all aspects of my life. From a very young age I have felt a strong inner force guiding me to help people to realise there is a supportive spiritual World available to them. Growing up, I was encouraged to try new things, to think and create for myself, to always have empathy for others and to make a positive difference in the World. When you look at how you can help the World you'll see many endless opportunities. I want you to have the simple spiritual tools available to you as mentioned in this book, to inspire you, to help you to laugh, to be happier, to know that you're never alone. You can find like-minded kindred spirits doing amazing things at the Spiritual Me community we are creating online at:

www.facebook.com/spiritualme101

www.spiritualme101.com

Jo Brothers lives a creative spiritual life and from an early age has written poems, stories and plays. She has found herself naturally moving into a career that connects together storytelling, communications and digital social media. In her spare time, she has written ten children's books that feature - The Extraordinary Tales of Queenie Alice Moon and The Adventures of Nano the Robot.

Visit Jo's websites for the latest inspiration, ideas, adventures and her blogs.

www.jobrothers.com or www.spiritualme101.com

Spiritual Me Series

Spiritual Me 101 – Advanced

Spiritual Me in Colour

Spiritual Me Cook Book

Spiritual Me for Teens

Organic Me

Goddess Me

Herbology Me

Celestial Me

Other Books

Cosmic Trick

~ Due out 2016 ~

Acknowledgements

I am blessed to have a large **#SpiritualMeSquad** with so many wonderful family members and friends. You've all played a part in bringing Spiritual Me the book to life and I'd like to profoundly thank and acknowledge: Sean, Wendy, Jane, John, Jason, Mike, Kris, Emma, Kate and Stella and the many supporting Angels in my life.

Only those who can see the invisible can do the impossible.
Albert Einstein

#SpiritualMeSquad is your support crew, team and network.

I used to think I was the strangest person in the World but then I thought there are so many people in the World, there must be someone just like me who feels bizarre and flawed in the same ways I do.

I would imagine her, and imagine that she must be out there thinking of me too. Well, I hope that if you are out there and read this and know that, yes, it's true I'm here, and I'm just as strange as you.

*‌**Frida Kahlo***

Table of Contents

About the Author 3
A Note to the Reader 9
You are the Secret 11
Getting Remapped 17
Consciousness 19
Ego 21
Spiritual Butler Consciousness 23
Karma Drama 25
HelpFull 27
Releasing Baggage 29
Writing to the Universe 31
The Light Engineer at Home 33
Plan Your Day 35
Inner Child 37
Colour Me 39
Technology Cleanse 41
Social Media 43
Chakras 45
Meditating 49
Manifesting and Intention Boards 51
Mantras and Intention Affirmations 53
Spiritual Me Intention Jar 55
Self-Love and Confidence 57
Soulmates and Love 59
Smells Divine 61
Candles 63
Crystals 65
Dreams 67
Connecting with the Archangels 69
Calling an Angel 71

Spiritual Me at Work 73
Injection of Light 77
Words have Power 81
Mercury in Retrograde 85
Message in a Book 87
Take Action 89
Goddess Power 91
Code 93
Super Power 95
Spiritual Me Intention Compass 97
Love Your Body 103
Spiritual Growth 105
A Final Word 107
Notes 109

A Note to the Reader

Endless incredible possibilities dwell within each and every one of us.

Jo Brothers

Hello, and welcome to Spiritual Me 101. There is no such thing as a coincidence so you have been divinely led here by the positive forces and Angels of the Universe. What is Spiritual Me? It is a user guide on how you can take care of yourself spiritually.

May this book bring you closer to you, your essence and your Soul and to equip you with some ideas and tools to help you navigate through life and the challenging stressful times we're currently living in. Increasingly psychologists and doctors are recognising a connection between spirituality, health, wellness, resiliency and mental strength. In high schools meditation is being introduced to assist students in dealing with exam stress.

To those of you who are brand new to spiritual themes and ideas, a huge welcome. Take it slowly, be true to you, and feel free to pick up and put down this book as often as you like. Life is not linear it is circular, so you don't need to read this book from cover to cover, you can choose what and when you'd like to read it.

To those of you who are walking a spiritual path, it is great to connect with you and thank you for reading this book.

The times we now live in are fast, busier and ever changing. You receive more information and data through news and advertisements in one week as compared with someone living in the early 1900's would have received in their entire lifetime. The fact that there is so much darkness in the World, means that we should all do as much as possible to create and share light, love, happiness and a positive attitude.

The more challenging the situation in which you find yourself, and the World, the greater the potential for more positivity, light and love. I believe we live in a World filled with possibilities and hope. We are One, we are all connected. The World has an abundance of good energy and love to go around but imagine how much more there would be if you could keep in a state of ever expanding consciousness of positivity, happiness and sharing. Being a force for good and love in the World.

This positive force is a part of us all and I believe in a loving Creator, call it the Universe, the Light, God, Buddha or whomever you believe in. I focus on gratitude, gratefulness and taking lessons from everything that comes my way.

Spiritual Me can assist you to connect to the inner you, your Soul, essence or spirit. Many of us have different aspects of ourselves that are more dominant during different stages of our day or week, such as Work Me, Home Me, Social Media Me, and then Spiritual Me - your Soul/Spirit.

Ideally being able to have the consciousness of your Soul/Spirit, Spiritual Me central to the decisions you make will lead you to having a more fulfilled and happier life. You can start with the intention of living a full happy life and being the cause for your own happiness and success, helping other people to be happy and achieve their goals, with you remaining PowerFull and full of energy. Remember the Universe always replenishes the energy you give away when sharing with others.

You are the Secret

Your Soul has infinite potential; never forget how powerfull you are. Allow yourself to discover your purpose.
Jo Brothers

The World you live in changes daily. The entire World is changing at a rapid rate and will continue to do so with the advancement in technologies and entire industries being disrupted and re-imagined. So it is important you know more about 'You', so that you can create a stable foundation for yourself and move forward fearlessly and help others on your journey.

Self-love and self-belief are an important foundation that you build on, to grow and develop. Love who you are now and Love who you will become. Deep down, or as a waking thought everyone wants to connect with their truest potential and their ultimate expression as a human being, which is to live as your authentic self.

Let me tell you a secret, an interesting fact about this book. I first started writing this book in 2004 and called it 'You are the Secret'. However, it remained unfinished and patiently waited for me to be 'ready' to complete and publish it.

So I do not know how many people the book could have helped had I finished it sooner. It could have been 3 or even 3 billion people? Waiting to get to the point where I felt I needed to write the book to help people like you, find the book 'Spiritual Me - A Practical Spiritual Guide For The Times We Live In'.

Let us help find the secret 'You within You' which is your Spiritual Me. You can not define yourself by comparing yourself with anyone else, you need to connect within, look inward and connect to your heart and Soul.

You are PowerFull (Full of Power)

Find a Meditation Space, somewhere you feel safe, where it is quiet to sit down and do this exercise. There are no wrong answers and write as much as you like for each question.

1. What are your passions? What lights you up when doing your job, hobby or being creative?

   _____
   _____
   _____

2. Who inspires you and why?

   _____
   _____
   _____

3. What are you good at and what are your strengths?

   _____
   _____
   _____

4. What environments do you like - Busy, City, Country, Home or Office?

5. What would you do if you knew you could not fail and how does it feel?

6. Are you ready to give up your time and money that you have now in order to try and bring it to life?

7. What is the special talent, gift, treasure that you have within you - your purpose/mission on how you are meant to share your light and Soul with the World?

8. Write a list of the top 10 people you love.

1.
2.
3.
4.
5.
6.
7.
8.
9.
10.

Did you include yourself on the list? I hope so.

Review your Answers

1. Congratulations! You will now know your Soul's purpose, your ideal environment, your think big aspirations, your commitment and your mission.

2. Now those of you who do know what you need to do you, you can start making plans, taking actions toward your goals, and taking little steps every day. This is how you will bring your life purpose into intention and manifest.

3. So as you reflect on your answers, did any surprise you? Explore these answers further in Meditation and ask for further guidance.

   - **Are you doing what inspires you?** Great, if you are. If you are not find a way to add inspiration into your life via online study, connecting with a group/organisation that inspires you. Start to re-imagine your life and slowly it will take form.

- If you realise you have an amazing idea, see how you could bring that idea to life.

- Perhaps you have realised you prefer a different work environment. Can you talk to your employer about a flexible work plan that would allow you work 1 day a week from home?

- There are always answers/solutions to any problem and at least 3 ways to achieve any goal.

4. If anything is not clear just yet, do not worry, start meditating and making the spiritual tools work for you until it is clear. Live in the moment and appreciate all that you have created in your life so far, and know that the best is yet to come.

You are wonderful just the way you are.
Jo Brothers

Getting Remapped

The secret of change is to focus all of your energy, not on fighting the old, but on building the new.
Socrates

Why do you get tests and obstacles in your life? You may ask, "**Why is this happening to me?**" or you may say, **"What is the spiritual reason this is happening to me, if the Universe/Creator/Light is looking after me, why am I on this emotional roller coaster?"**

You have said or thought this at some stage in your life as a curve ball hits you from out of nowhere. It could be having to move house unexpectedly, having to find a new job after your company restructured or the ending of a relationship or marriage or a medical challenge.

The answer, it happened so that you can rise up and overcome it and reveal the potential light within you as you will be stronger after for having experienced the challenge. I am not saying it is always easy, however it is important to maintain your certainty that everything will improve and get better. Maintain your inner peace and to stay happy and do not let your Ego drag you into doubt or depression, which does not help you always Focus on the good.

The truth is your life will now have more LIGHT, blessings and opportunities than you have had prior to these testing times.

You are human, so if you fall and get upset, know that when you rise again, having conquered a huge inner battle, you and your consciousness will be stronger, lighter and a lot wiser for the experience and a good thing will happen.

Consciousness

Consciousness is your Soul, your life force, your spark, your energy intelligence, awareness, potential, luminosity and talent.

Jo Brothers

Right now all around the World many people are living an unfulfilling nonspiritual life tied to a materialistic World, with their experiences anchored in the realm of our five senses. Being sight, smell, taste, touch and hearing, with our Ego having a big say in what goes on. Yet we are all by nature spiritual and if you are intuitive and have a sixth sense, you could also be receiving the messages as clairaudient (hearing), clairvoyant (seeing), clairsentient (feeling) and claircognisant (knowing) and there are many others.

So what is Consciousness?

It is Awareness.

It is you, your Soul, your life force, your spark, your energy intelligence, awareness, potential, luminosity and talent.

When we say affirmations or mantras, we are asking to create this consciousness for ourselves, which will help to create it in our lives. That is why it is so important to focus on positive thoughts and ideas, as it literally affects our life. For example:

"I am safe and have a strong foundation that supports me to excel in life. I am confident and bold in my actions, Soul and spirit, as my life is loving and stable."

So, as you connect daily to being more aware of connecting to being aware, you will make more decisions from your Soul consciousness that is guided by the heart and love. You will look more to sharing your time and talents to help others and feel infinite possibilities.

You will begin to feel more and more comfortable with who you are and you will be operating on an outlook of love, to the point where you do not feel you are pushing or striving to manifest or to create your life, but rather allowing your potential to come into being a success in your life.

Meditation is the key to connecting with your consciousness so you can activate the potential, light, gifts, talents and inner super power within you.

Ego

Ego is the naughty Angel trying to stop your Soul excelling and shining bright.

Jo Brothers

You have an Ego, we all do. Sometimes your Ego tells you, you are better and sometimes your Ego tells you, you are not good enough. It is the negative voice in your head that makes you feel, **"It is me against the World!"**, **"It is not fair!!"**, **"I am not good enough!"**, "**I can not succeed!"**, **"Poor me!"**, **"Why me?"**

Have you ever had a conversation going on in your head that you did not start? Yes, that is your Ego. Or a random thought pops into your mind about someone who annoyed you, say five years ago. Yes, again that is your Ego, a big distraction that you can learn to tune out or at least become aware that it is not your thoughts.

The Ego wants you to remain stuck in your present situation, whatever that is and not to evolve into your awesome unique potential, stopping you from being able to share your gift with the World. Many of you may be thinking, **'I really love my life and I am successful and happy'**; all I am saying is that wherever you are, there is a next level of happiness, fulfillment, success, love - in fact infinite potential.

Now that you are aware of your Ego, you can start to see when your Ego turns up to try and make decisions for you and to lead you down the wrong path and all the while wanting to waste your precious time so that you do not focus on your infinite potential and unique greatness and how to be a force for good in the World. So let us get some help from our Spiritual Butler Consciousness.

Spiritual Butler Consciousness

Think it, Make it, Do it, Own it.

Jo Brothers

Spiritual Butler Consciousness is also called Certainty.

What if you all had a Spiritual Butler? An internal helpful concierge that would identify and greet every negative Ego thought you have with a **"Hello, sorry your name is not on the list you will have to leave."** Much like consciousness or mindfulness, where you are conscious or aware of something that is happening to you in the now, in the present moment, acknowledging it is happening to you and moving on. Mindfulness is considered to be a meditative state which can assist you to handle issues/challenges in a stress free way.

You can use your internal Spiritual Butler Consciousness Certainty within you, that is able to get you into the boxing ring without any thoughts of Fear. Fear, also known as, Pain, Emptiness, Unfairness, Feelings of Isolation or Abandonment or even Alienation.

Your Spiritual Butler Consciousness is activated and strengthened every day when you chose to be Proactive instead of Reactive. When you chose to rise to the challenge and not fall into Victim Mentality, you are taking a calculated risk to bring your dreams to life.

You can draw on the tools I talk about in this book and in my experience my Spiritual Butler Consciousness/Certainty grows stronger when I help other people in their lives, overcome a challenge and help them with their journey. It grows stronger when you share your time and/or money, when you would rather be doing something for yourself.

Some people say Fear is good and that it pushes them. That is probably true if they have already been able to overcome many challenges and know that they can do it! For those starting the journey of overcoming Fear if you can remember one thing, remember:

Fear is a liar and the minute you stand up to it, it disappears, it runs away and vanishes.

Karma Drama

Every second of the day we create positive or negative energy that will return to us. Make sure you create more positive energy, it not only helps you, it helps the World.

Jo Brothers

Have you ever felt as if everything is falling apart around you and as you fix one issue or drama in your life another one springs up? Sometimes that is the Universe preparing something better for you and sometimes it is something you need to experience in order to grow from that experience.

Karma or the law of cause and effect exists; it is real and one of the Spiritual Laws of the Universe. What you put out into the Universe is exactly what you will get reflected back to you. So if you want Love in your life, give Love! If you want to receive, then Give! Sometimes you need to give and give and give, in order to receive. So, you need to be able to 'Let Go!' of the outcome while being patient with the amount of time it takes.

There are Spiritual Laws that exist and much like driving a car, you need to know the road rules. Karma and/or cause and effect travels with you across lifetimes. So, sometimes you need to be extra patient while the energies around you change and transform.

You are able to call on the assistance of Angels at any time and invite them into your life to help you with specific issues you may have. You can talk to them in your mind or out loud and they will be able to help you and an infinite number of people at the same time. So don't worry you are not disturbing the Angels and they can help you anytime.

- **Ariel** guardian of animals and nature, healing, love and creative energy.

- **Chamuel** guardian of unconditional love, emotional healing, romantic love and Soulmates.

- **Gabriel** guardian of communication, transformation, change and emotion.

- **Daniel** guardian of spiritual guidance, your Soul's life purpose, intuition, strength, willpower and courage.

- **Jophiel** guardian of joy, creativity, liberation and education.

- **Michael** guardian of protection, strength, empowerment and compassion.

- **Raguel** guardian of justice and harmony.

- **Raphael** guardian of healing, science, learning/knowledge and oneness.

- **Raziel** guardian allowing access to the secrets of the Universe and your Soul.

- **Uriel** guardian of unconditional love, overcoming difficult challenges and achieving balance.

- **Zadkiel** guardian of compassion, love and forgiveness.

HelpFull

Help others to succeed and success will flow to you.
Jo Brothers

Karma or call it cause and effect, means that whatever you put out into the Universe will come back to you eventually.

When you help another person, you are creating circular energy in conjunction with the Universe that will help that person you are helping and it also helps you. In fact it is said that the fastest way to help manifest your desires is to help another person manifest their dreams and desires.

So as an example, say a friend has a dream to open a retail store and asks you for help on their first week of opening. It is a big stretch for you, uncomfortable in fact as you do not have much time for yourself, however if you do this, you are creating important seeds for manifesting your own desires. The harder it is for you to help, whether you are time poor or cash poor, the greater the energy that will return to you.

Imagine a World where everyone helped each other's dreams come true! As we are all unique individuals, all 7.3 Billion of us, there are unique things we have all come here to do.

Energy never disappears, so if you invest hours or years into a relationship or project and it does not work out, do not worry the Universe has that energy in storage for you, to support you in another relationship or project. Energy can not be lost so nothing is lost.

Releasing Baggage

Old challenges or karma that no longer serves you. You have learnt the lesson now let go to allow new energy and opportunities to flow to you.

Jo Brothers

Yes we all have it, now let us look at releasing the correct suitcase and remember, do not stumble over something behind you. Which means do not worry about past mistakes just start making positive new actions.

Once upon an online spending spree a young woman realised she had incurred credit card debt and decided she wanted to pay this off as soon as possible and release this karma drama baggage from her life forever.

This meant less going out with her friends, and more crafting up ways to pay the debt back. In fact she decided to do volunteer work to help others and to inject the energy of compassion into her life. In doing so she met her future husband through this work, along with many wonderful new friends more in tune with her desire to share and pay it forward in the World. So the debt had delivered her a challenge and an opportunity with a miracle as well.

Ultimately, she realised she needed to ask to release her baggage which was an unhealthy relationship to money and spending it recklessly. Once she did that the money would flow to her as money is energy and now she could manage the energy in the correct way. When you are sent a huge burden/challenge it is to reveal your potential and great light.

Where is your baggage? If you do not know where your baggage is you can ask a trusted friend or loved one to give you their feedback in a loving way. Remember to explain to them that you want to make some major changes to your Karma Drama and could they please help you, ask them.

Where are you stuck? You want to see where you are stuck in your life and why you keep making the same mistakes.

Do you need to forgive? That would mean you need to release the energy of unforgiveness.

Do you need to step up? That would mean you need to release the energy associated to self-sabotage.

Do you need to be happier? Try writing lists expressing your thanks and gratitude for all that you have.

Do you need to stop judging others? This could mean you need to develop a greater level of self-love. If you are harsh on yourself, then you are harsh towards others.

Writing to the Universe

There are subtle body energies/imprints in this World and the energy can shift and be released when you write a letter to let go of any hurt or upset that happened in the past with a specific person or place.

Jo Brothers

If you have issues/problems that you would like to release you can write a letter to the Universe. Write openly and honestly and do not hold back as this letter is not going to actually be sent, instead you are going to burn this letter.

Begin your letter with **"Dear Universe..."** and then write for as long as you feel the need. Be open and release all your fears and pain as no one will read this letter apart from you. When you are finished do not read the letter as the purpose of writing this letter is to release this energy out of you and to free you from any anger, hurt, fear etc. Prepare to burn the letter safely in a fireplace or similar.

Similarly if someone you know has hurt you, and you have anger and would like to release this, you may write a letter addressed to whom you have the issue with, again write freely and at the completion of the letter you can then burn it.

Now know that you have released these feelings and you can affirm this out loud, by saying: **"I forgive (insert name) and wish them well"**.

Sometimes you're holding onto feelings of unforgiveness and you think that by doing so it is going to 'correct' an injustice, however that is not the case and the only person being hurt and blocked from your potential is you.

Invite the Angels into your life and ask them to surround you with the energy of protection and to help guide you daily.

- **Ariel** guardian of animals and nature, healing, love and creative energy.

- **Chamuel** guardian of unconditional love, emotional healing, romantic love and Soulmates.

- **Gabriel** guardian of communication, transformation, change and emotion.

- **Daniel** guardian of spiritual guidance, your Soul's life purpose, intuition, strength, willpower and courage.

- **Jophiel** guardian of joy, creativity, liberation and education.

- **Michael** guardian of protection, strength, empowerment and compassion.

- **Raguel** guardian of justice and harmony.

- **Raphael** guardian of healing, science, learning/knowledge and oneness.

- **Raziel** guardian allowing access to the secrets of the Universe and your Soul.

- **Uriel** guardian of unconditional love, overcoming difficult challenges and achieving balance.

- **Zadkiel** guardian of compassion, love and forgiveness.

The Light Engineer at Home

Love begins at home and it is not how much we do, but how much love we put in that action.
Mother Teresa

A Light Engineer at home is the primary caregiver, Mother, Father or person in charge or friends sharing a home, also known as a CEO of the home; however we can all help to create a home filled with light and a supportive home environment.

The energy in a home is crucial for the nurture and support of the entire family and requires a lot of energy. So imagine if every time you do any action or chore at home you are injecting positivity and excitement that will create positivity around you and the home. For example, inject love by washing dishes, do housekeeping or cleaning.

To connect to more energy and light in our homes know that every time you light a candle you are drawing pure energy into your home and living environment.

Fresh flowers, plants and scented candles or essential oils and incense energise the energy in the home, and draw positive angels and energies.

Depending on your personal style you may like sleek, minimalist furniture and decor at home or alternatively, you may prefer a collection of bright colours and comfort, all are equally great.

What you do need to be aware of is 'clutter'. When you are finished with something, give it away, rehome it, recycle it or throw it away. You need to ensure your home and work environments only have items that you use, want and are functional.

So if you have just read this and are thinking about a spare room at home that needs a tidy, or a wardrobe that needs to be cleared out to be shared with new owners you should do that now.

Your home is your sacred space, so make sure you have clean and uncluttered surroundings to ensure you have clear energy all around you that can support you to manifest your dreams, goals and intentions.

Plan Your Day

People spend more time planning a holiday than planning their life. Imagine if we planned our days, lives, careers and spiritual development with the same commitment.
Jo Brothers

Building a routine that supports you and sets you up in the best way for your day needs some planning. You need to try and start the day in the most fulfilling, calm and spiritually supportive way. You will be awakening yourself to a World filled with new possibilities every day.

So you hear the alarm go off in the morning, it is time to wake up. You turn the alarm off that hopefully is not a phone? As sleeping with phones or tablets in the bedroom is not the best spiritual environment for restful sleep. Remember looking at your phone stimulates the brain making it harder to get to sleep. You can buy an alarm clock.

Here is a suggested method on how you could plan out your day, with you trying this one day per week or every day. If you have any children and/or care for any elderly parents, see if you are able to move around the exercise time.

3 Steps in 5 Minutes

1. Wake up.

2. Take some time to properly wake up and feel the energy of appreciation and gratitude for your life and everything that you have.

3. Quick Meditation (2-5 minutes). Consciously breathe in and out several times, appreciate the new morning, and give thanks for being alive and move on to setting your intention for the day of what you want to accomplish or focus on. For example, **"Today I will have productive meetings and meet one new person I can network**

and work together with or they become a great friend. I appreciate my life and blessings and pass it forward by sharing with others. I will remain positive and remember that every obstacle is an opportunity to learn." Feel free to write your own intention affirmation and check our website for more examples on www.spiritualme101.com.

Additional steps if you have time

4. In the morning if you have got the time to go to the gym, do yoga, swim, walk the dog or play tennis, this is an excellent time of the day to fit this in and is a great time to think and get ideas for your projects at home or work. Exercise is a great release

5. Breakfast can include a soothing green juice, green tea or stimulating coffee, it is up to you.

Create your own Spiritual Me Morning Intention

"Today I will radiate positivity and love to everyone I meet. I connect to my Soul and start the journey to reveal and share with the World my potential and gifts."

At www.spiritualme101.com we will be posting ideas for morning intentions and we would love to hear yours. So please post your morning intentions on our Facebook Page www.facebook.com/spiritualme101 or via Instagram @spiritualme101 - #spiritualmemorningintention

Inner Child

Imagine if we had the same attitude a child has - nothing is a problem, we get up and start again quickly, we love our friends within minutes of a disagreement and we are forever curious.
Jo Brothers

Let us talk about your inner child, your creative side, the part of you that loves to play, watch a great movie, listen to music, run fast in the wind, play sports, give and receive a hug, find a fabulous new dress and shoes (dressing up for grown up's) and the list goes on.

Your Inner Child is also the part of you connected to fun, creativity, innovation, the energy of resilience and trying new things. In the times we are living in, many people's Inner Child has definitely come out to play.

With all the traumatic things you are witnessing in the news and around the World it is understandable that sometimes you may feel helpless and weighed down with negativity. However, please know that by connecting with your Inner Child and keeping your creativity flowing, you can invent or create something wonderful that can influence the entire World to a happier, lighter time. It has been documented that adults suffering from stress drew peace, comfort and healing from a simple task of colouring in an adult picture book. Sometimes you need to calm yourself and come back to your center of gravity and feel focused from the labyrinth and constant chatter and worry that goes on in your mind.

It is important to remind your Inner Child that there is always good happening all around the World. That there are always people helping others and that there are adults and children doing incredible things to help each other and their communities.

Even when you feel tired, and hopeless there are miracles happening all around the World, and that someone somewhere has just invented an advance in medicine that can save the lives of millions of people. Communities around the World, families, friends and care givers, are all working together to create new pathways of hope and positivity. People are donating and helping people and animals in need.

Imagination has led to so many of the amazing advancements helping humanity today. Stay forever young and resilient and nurture your inner child. ☺

Play is the highest form of research.
Albert Einstein

Colour Me

Each one of us has a unique vibrant and colourful Soul.
Jo Brothers

Colouring in, is a relaxing colourful expression of your emotions into the physical. It activates your creative energy and you are really meditating in colour. All colours have different energy and relate to your chakra colours and also to crystals.

On the next page you'll find a colouring in image for you to colour in.

We would love to see your end result and suggest you take a photo and send it to us via any of the following social media platforms:

- Post to our **Facebook** page at

    - www.facebook.com/spiritualme101

    - it's @spiritualme101

- Post to our **Instagram** page at
- www.instagram.com/spiritualme101
- it's @spiritualme101 - #spiritualmesquad
  - #spiritualme
  - #spiritualme101

or email us at:

- social@spiritualme101.com

SPIRITUAL ME

Technology Cleanse

Create some tech free, Wi-Fi free, data free time for you and your loved ones. Time that is real face to face and heart to heart conversations.

Jo Brothers

I absolutely recommend doing a technology cleanse, detox or whatever you would like to call it. I recently did a 3-day technology mini break and found myself feeling calmer and 100 times more creative. My life and career requires me to be contactable and able to read emails and connect online daily which is true for many of us.

So it makes sense to take frequent breaks. You would not watch TV 24/7 straight or listen to music non-stop? So it makes sense to give yourself a break if and when you can.

As a good friend of mine, who happens to be 19, said to me recently **"Jo when I get together with my cousins, we are putting our phones in a bag and putting them away for the weekend, it is family time not Wi-Fi time!"**

Be present, and totally focused on the conversations and experiences you are having with the people in your life. Allow yourself a break from being 'always on' digitally.

Another positive effect of having a technology cleanse is to give you a break from the intensity and ferocity of the daily news. What I mean is that if there has been a god forbid tragic event in the World, the images and stories are shared multiple times on every major blog or news site. They then share the same images and story multiple times on social networking sites, so that you get to the point where you are on your phone swiping through agonising stories 10 times over. This is traumatic and heart-breaking since you merely went online to grab a recipe or see a photo from a friend. If there are donation pages set up to help the tragedy, you can support those in need by donating and/or by praying for them. I personally always light a candle and pray for every situation or tragedy I hear about. Prayer always helps, as well as donating to support the supporters.

Many times you did not choose or seek out to have these heartbreaking images bombard your senses. Looking at these types of stories on repeat will make you feel depressed and/or helpless.

An algorithm is generated by data and that data is the number of people interacting with a particular story. There are positive things happening in the World and they don't always make it to the top of an algorithm. So depending on a number of factors, including what your friends are looking at, your daily digital experience is often not actually of your own choosing or intention. So be kind to yourself and take a few days off with a technology cleanse when you can.

Social Media

Create or find the good and amplify that out. The World needs to see and share more positive stories.
Jo Brothers

Everything we do, think, write and speak has energy and the same goes for sharing a comment or post on Social Media and the Internet.

If you want to add positive energy to the World, I recommend you only share or re-share content that is positive, helps get a message out for a fundraiser or organisation and tells a great story of someone's personal achievements and so on.

When enough of us tune our consciousness to positive intentions and messages we start a ripple effect.

At www.facebook.com/spiritualme101 we share uplifting, positive, happy filled content which we are happy for you to re-share.

Chakras

Chakras are the colourful powerhouses of energy flowing in your body and the energy you radiate.
Jo Brothers

Our body has seven main energy centres (spiritual power/levels of body consciousness) that run along our spinal column, from the top of our head to the base of our spine, called Chakras. Chakra is a Hindi word that means 'wheel or wheel of spinning energy'.

Asian cultures have used the Chakras for healing for hundreds of years and, in fact, Yoga connects to the Chakra system and teaches how to activate and clear the Chakras.

The seven Chakras or energy centres in our bodies relate to specific areas of our body and are associated with emotional or subtle energies that can affect how you feel and behave.

Chakras have different colours and you can use colour light healing, such as Reiki or Aura Soma together with crystals and sound to rebalance your energy. When working with clearing or strengthening your Chakras ask the Angel Doctor, Archangel Raphael to join you.

- **Violet** in colour is the **1st Chakra** in the Crown area.
- **Indigo** in colour is the **2nd Chakra** in the Third Eye area (middle of forehead).
- **Blue** in colour is the **3rd Chakra** in the Throat area.
- Green in colour is the **4th Chakra** in the Heart area.
- in colour is the **5th Chakra** in the Solar Plexus area (stomach).
- Orange in colour is the **6th Chakra** in the Sacral area (also know as the navel).
- Red in colour is the **7th Chakra** in the Root area (at the base of the spine).

Chakra	#	Positive Intention
The Crown	1	I am at one with the universe and my soul
The Third Eye	2	I trust my intuition
The Throat	3	I express myself with love and openness
The Heart	4	I send and receive love
The Solar Plexus	5	I am confident, strong and powerful
The Sacral	6	I live my life full of passion
The Root	7	I am safe and supported in my life

Chakras and Positive Intentions

Meditating

Often we think were too 'busy' to meditate and when we do find the time to meditate we realise that we need to be 'busy' with our daily meditation.
Jo Brothers

I love that quote and it is quite relevant to the times we are living in with much of our time being 'busy'. So, 5–20 minutes will be fine and you can extend your meditation whenever you have the time.

1. Establish a safe special meditation space at home where you can meditate and you should always use this safe space when meditating at home. This is so that the energy and atmosphere will develop and your mind will feel relaxed in this space and you will be able to easily meditate whenever you want to. You can light a candle or incense to create a warm energy and there is also some great music for meditating to, so check out our YouTube channel.

2. Timing is crucial and you need a time in your day when your mind is not too busy. So when you wake up or go to sleep are excellent times.

3. Consistency, doing the meditation at the same time every day will help to create a pattern and you can easily connect to the meditative state quicker with the familiarity of time and location.

4. Generally, it is suggested to sit on a chair or sofa with your feet flat on the floor and your arms in a resting state with your eyes closed. You can also sit on the floor cross-legged; I have also found it just as easy lying down. It is a personal choice and I suggest you experiment and see what works best for you.

5. Start doing some breathing to open up your chest and lungs. Breathe in and hold for 3 seconds and exhale, repeat that 3 times.

6. Sit still a moment and empty your mind of any thoughts that you do not want. So you can be ready to experience a clearing or meditative conversation with yourself. Allow a few minutes for this to happen.

7. Try to stay awake and remain calm focusing on your breathing and just release the day and all worries and doubts.

8. Affirm one of your life goals, for example, **"I am safe, I am strong, I am creative, I am prosperous, I am in perfect health, I am in a committed relationship with my Soulmate."**

9. Write meditations relating to your Chakras (refer to the Chakra chart) or where you are holding pain, for example, your lower back, Root Chakra - **"I am safe and have a strong foundation that supports me to excel at life. I am confident and bold in my actions, Soul and spirit as my life is loving and stable."**

10. Now you can ask a question and wait to hear an answer.

Check out www.spiritualme101.com for some meditation music to help you.

Manifesting and Intention Boards

I am safe, I am strong, and I am creative, healthy and prosperous as I create miracles with the Universe. My intention is to be a force of good in the World.

Jo Brothers

So you have decided you want a change, a new life, home, career, success, so I would recommend creating a mood/desire board and a great place to do this is online at www.pinterest.com. You can set up an account and create a private board to share with your partner in life, love or business or get some magazines and find images to cut and paste to create your Manifesting and Intention boards on cardboard or in a large journal. We all have a unique and powerful way for ourselves and our Soul's essence to be expressed and manifested, so remember to add a spiritual dimension to your intention boards.

The Universe and your personal destiny will most likely be far greater than you can visualise just yet, so stay open to infinite possibilities and wait for the Universe to start delivering you these messages. Your potential will be greater than you can imagine, so get comfortable with connecting to real crazy big goals.

Setting up and pinning or pasting images that reflect what you would like to manifest in your life is not enough. Your intention and holding the visualisation is the key. Remember you are activating the energy that already exists within you. You need to 'be' in the space where it has already happened and you have done it. You already have the fulfillment shown on your mood/desire board.

You need to embody and literally feel as if your wish has already been made manifest and that it has happened. For example, you already see yourself as:

- Happily married to your Soulmate,
- Happily living with your life partner
- CEO of a successful company
- CEO of your own successful company
- An entrepreneur
- Prosperity in health and wealth
- As a mother or father in a loving family
- Healthy, fit and in perfect health
- Living in a beautiful house which is also a loving home
- Inventing or creating a new brand or business
- Having a regular income

It is done, you have it all!

Now this will take practice and I consider this to be no different than the time you would invest into meditation, or connecting to any of the other tools I have mentioned in this book. Your mind is consciousness, so for you to visualise your goals takes you into the life state that you would like in the 'now'.

Mantras and Intention Affirmations

Every day we start again. So every day tell yourself that today is the day I will rise and start the journey toward my greatness.
Jo Brothers

I believe that a positive thought and intention has more power than a negative thought and I practice this philosophy in my life. You can use positive thoughts to create them and attract more positive life experiences for yourself as the Universe responds to your actions.

Positive Intention Affirmations

- I now give myself permission to be loving, sharing and to reach my full potential.

- I am a force of Love and send this out into the World and see it reflected back to me.

- I am connected and in tune with my inner power at all times.

- I am permanently free of fear now and always.

- I ignite the feeling of urgency in achieving my Soul's purpose and I acknowledge I may feel uncomfortable which is a sign that I am on the right path.

- I am positive and have intuitive creative consciousness which allows me to connect to my potential now and always.

- Love, Unity, Abundance, Humility, Sharing and Oneness are mine now that Ego does not exist.

- Everything I am seeking is now seeking me.

- I am safe and capable of anything and everything that I imagine.

- I am healthy in all ways; every cell in my body is filled with endless, infinite light.

- I am always learning, growing and connected to my Soul's plan.

- I create and make my dreams come true with ease.

- I always surround myself with magical, sparkle heart shaped balls of Love, Healing and Protection.

- I see and experience the World around me through a lens of Love and return this energy out into the World.

- I have absolute certainty that I will achieve all my goals and I will help others and radiate this energy of oneness into the World.

- All my needs are met and exceeded.

- I feel so good. (repeated 100 times)

- I awaken the Goddess within me.

Spiritual Me Intention Jar

Our consciousness is our reality, so connect to your intention of being the ultimate force of good for the World.

Jo Brothers

My Spiritual Me Intention Jar

Alongside your Intention Boards you may want to create an Intention Jar or Vessel. All you will need is an empty jar or container with a lid and some paper and pen.

As you have read throughout this book, an Intention means that you are setting a goal that you intend to achieve. So, once you have a list of your Intentions written out, they are ready to go into your Intention Jar.

Light a scented candle and read your Intentions out loud and visualise them as already existing, as if you have already achieved the Intentions. You can also add some 'bling and sparkle' to your Intention Jar by adding glitter or crystals to super change your Intention Jar.

You can add Intentions to your Intention Jar at any time and once you have achieved one of the goals or mastered the consciousness, acknowledge this and give thanks.

To get you started, here are some examples of Positive Intention Affirmations

- There is peace and harmony in the World.

- Everyone on the planet has enough food to eat and a place to call home.

- I am connected to my life purpose.

- I am open to receive messages from the Universe to help mankind.

- I am supported by all the energy of the Universe to achieve my goals.

- I am in the best job, house, relationship that suits my Soul's evolution right now.

- I am in a loving relationship with my Soulmate/life partner.

Self-Love and Confidence

Today I will radiate positivity and love to everyone I meet, including myself. I connect to my Soul and start the journey to reveal and share with the World my potential and gifts.

Jo Brothers

Self-Love can be a bit tricky to get your head around. Self-Love does not mean you have a huge Ego. Self-Love is the love and acceptance you have for you, your Soul, your body, your talents, your issues and the journey you are on. It is the 'whole package'!

Know that you and everyone on the planet has a spark of divine light inside of them and everyone has a unique life purpose to share their talent, their essence with the World.

Perfect does not exist, perfect means that exactly where you are in your life is perfect for you as you connect to your potential to become the best you can be. The challenges and the joys are part of the journey you are on.

As an example, today all companies need to move quickly and innovate to keep relevant in a constantly changing World. They understand that part of moving forward is to understand that perfection is in the process and evolution. How many technology products, cars or planes look the same as they did 10, 20 or even 30 years ago?

There are more people on this planet unaware of their greatness than there are those bragging about how great they are. The majority of the World suffers from a LACK of Self-Love and Self Belief. Know that you make a difference and the World needs you to come alive with Love.

Know and repeat

- I am safe and have a strong foundation that supports me to excel at life.

- I am confident and bold in my actions, Soul and spirit, as my life is loving and stable.

- I am open to receiving all the blessings the Universe has for me.

Soulmates and Love

Unconditional Love, Romantic Love, Love is Love and that is the fibre that holds our World together. Be a conduit of Love and radiate Love.

Jo Brothers

Firstly, I wish that everyone wanting to be reunited with their Soulmate may merit this blessing as soon as possible.

Ok, so yes it is true. You will most likely meet your Soulmate once you are living your own fun, fulfilling life and you will most likely, literally find them appearing in your life beside you. Your Soulmate is likely to have similar interests and passions and you will meet your Soulmate amongst like-minded people. So, live your passions, hobbies, travel, take courses, volunteer, socialise and enjoy life!

If you have had an idea to attend a class either kung fu or cooking, then take this as a quiet whisper from the Universe that you should in fact do this. Not one but two of my girlfriends booked a flight to a city they had never been to before. They had a feeling this was something they needed to do and as it turns out both of them met their Soulmate on that trip from taking that leap of faith and arriving in a new city.

Soulmates may not only be romantic, they could also be a close friend, mentor, family member, neighbour or boss and as you are reading this people may come to mind and you will know that they are in your heart, whether they live across town or across the globe.

Soulmates whether romantic or not, are people we are meant to connect to and in some way make the World a better place or do a project/business together.

Romantic Soulmates push each other towards their greatness. So a relationship that is growing and developing everyday will still have times where you may disagree. But at the core of your relationship you will have the same goals, morals and a love that allows you both to express your truth, to be able to speak openly and be vulnerable with each other.

Smells Divine

Angels are drawn to areas that smell beautiful, fresh and vibrant. Invite them into your home with candles, oils, flowers and perfume.

Jo Brothers

Let us look into the spectrum of aromatherapy oils that you can use to stimulate the energy in your home and that will also create positive energetic reactions within your body. You can get an oil burner that plugs into the electric wall socket and has a safe low heat that activates the scents of the oils or you can get an oil burner powered by tea light candles. Oils can be purchased as blended scents or a scent on its own, like Rose fragrance.

- **Ginger** is a powerful positive warm upbeat spicy scent great for overall health and wellbeing.

- **Jasmine** is calming, stimulates confidence, optimism and feelings of renewal and reduces the feeling of fear.

- **Lavender** has calming properties, heals emotional stress and assists with headaches, nerves and sleep.

- **Lemon** is calming, helps to get clarity when feeling anxious, nervous and exhausted, is an energy booster.

- **Mandarin** many claim has the most refreshing, calming and uplifting smell with positive energy and it's also great to help with peaceful sleep.

- **Orange** is a warm, bright powerful scent that reminds you of the sun and optimism.

- **Patchouli** is excellent for stressed busy minds with an earthy aroma that helps to ease feelings of anxiety.

- **Peppermint** is used to clear sinuses, stimulates clear thinking, concentration and is an all-round energy booster/invigorator.

- **Sandalwood** is a wonderful scent to assist with meditation, relaxing the body and increased concentration.

- **Ylang Ylang** is a mood elevator, calming and relaxing, an intoxicating heavy floral aroma with a reputation in history of being an aphrodisiac.

Candles

Lighting candles draws light into your home or wherever you may be.

Jo Brothers

Candles (both wax and oil) have been around since at least 3000 BC. The word candle is derived from the Latin word 'candera'. It is said that the flame on a candle represents Soul, spirit and the source of creation.

Candles are no longer our main source of light however they still play a central role in our lives at times of celebration, holidays, birthdays, weddings, prayer, and connection, casting a warm glow in homes, stores and events.

As mentioned previously candles are great to have in your home to inject energy and light into the environment. Equally scented diffusers are wonderful too. My home is filled with scented candles and diffusers creating a wonderful perfume that emanates throughout the house. I love the scent of Vanilla, French Pear, Rose and Peony and in fact most flowers as well as blends of deep wood and cinnamon.

- **Communication** is enhanced by the aroma of Vanilla.
- **Creativity** is enhanced by the aroma of Jasmine, Lotus, Saffron and Sandalwood.
- **Harmony, Love and Forgiveness** are enhanced by the aroma of Apple, Pine, Rose, Rosewood and Ylang Ylang.
- **Intuition** is enhanced by the aroma of Cinnamon, Geranium, Lavender and Rosemary.
- **Money and Success** are enhanced by the aroma of Almond, Cinnamon, Ginger and Honeysuckle.

- **Protection and Wellbeing** are enhanced by the aroma of Angelica, Coconut, Frankincense, Gardenia, Lilac and sandalwood.

- **Revitalise Energy** is enhanced by the aroma of Vanilla.

Did you know that a candle's flame does not have a shadow - it is all light.

Crystals

Crystals are healing objects, jewellery and miracles from mother Earth that conduct and activate energy.
Jo Brothers

Crystals have been used for thousands of years as healing objects, jewelry and have served as conductors for us to activate the energy inside us or to clear energies from within. Coming from deep within Mother Earth they have pure energy contained within them.

Crystals work on several levels for you, either mentally or emotionally and/or physically. So you can have Crystals around you at home, in your bedroom, you can wear them as rings, bracelets or necklaces. You can also carry Crystals for confidence.

How can Crystals help you?

Let's look at the attributes that Crystals have and pair them with what you are seeking to connect with and draw into your life or to heal. Remember that some Crystals have multiple healing properties and every Archangel is also associated with a Crystal.

- **Body (Blood, Heart, Eyes, lungs)** are helped by Bloodstone Crystals.

- **Communicating** is helped by Celestite Crystals.

- **Connecting to Angels** is helped by Angelite, Celestite and Moonstone Crystals.

- **Feminine Body Cycles in Harmony** are helped by Moonstone Crystals.

- **Healing** is helped by Amethyst, Clear Quartz, Moldavite and Opal Crystals.

- **Life Purpose** is helped by Clear Quartz Crystals.

- **Love and Soulmates** are helped by Pink Tourmaline and Rose Quartz Crystals.

- **Money, Prosperity and Confidence** are helped by Citrine Crystals.

- **Pregnancy** is helped by Rose Quartz Crystals.

- **Reducing Stress** is helped by Blue Topaz and Turquoise Crystals.

Dreams

Dreams can be a bridge to events yet to come in our lives. The more positive actions we make every day the clearer and truer the messages in our dreams will be.

__Jo Brothers__

Dreams are absolutely a connection to your consciousness and you can receive messages in your dreams. If you would like to ask for a message you can try this tool and you do not need to be psychic to do this. You are looking to access your higher self-awareness in the World of consciousness.

- Get a small piece of paper and write down the name of the Person/Angel you would like to ask a question from and put it under your pillow. For example, "**Archangel Michael what shall I do about my work situation?**" or **"Archangel Michael what can you tell me about my life purpose?"**

In order to have dreams, you need a restful night's sleep. I know I am sounding like your Mother now, however this will mean:

- Having acted positively throughout the day.
- Having a tidy and de-cluttered bedroom.
- Having fresh air/oxygen coming into the bedroom.
- Having the bedroom dark enough so you can easily fall asleep.
- Removing all devices, tablets and phones from the bedroom.
- Playing some peaceful and calming music.
- Having flowers and/or a plant in the room.

You are now ready to lie down, go to sleep and hopefully you will wake up with an answer. Remember dreams are often cryptic, so write down your dreams and wait for the message to become clear to you. If you do not get an answer try and repeat the process until you do get a message or move on and try another tool that may work better for you, like meditation.

You may like to start keeping a journal of all your dreams. A 'dream factory' with many dreams giving you inspiration and guidance in your daily life.

Connecting with the Archangels

Open your heart, ask an Angel for help and remember to notice the messages they will send you through the voice of a stranger, an online article or a song. So be open to truly hearing the answers.

Jo Brothers

1. Establish a safe special meditation space at home where you can meditate and you should always use this safe space when meditating at home. This is so that the energy and atmosphere will develop and your mind will feel relaxed in this space and you will be able to easily meditate whenever you want to. You can light a candle or incense to create a warm energy and there is also some great music for meditating to, so check out our YouTube channel.

2. Timing is crucial and you need a time in your day when your mind is not too busy. So when you wake up or go to sleep are excellent times. I recommend you put aside 15–30 minutes for this meditation.

3. Consistency, doing the meditation at the same time every day will help to create a pattern and you can easily connect to the meditative state quicker with the familiarity of time and location.

4. Generally, it is suggested to sit on a chair or sofa with your feet flat on the floor and your arms in a resting state with your eyes closed. You can also sit on the floor cross-legged; I have also found it just as easy lying down. It is a personal choice and I suggest you experiment and see what works best for you.

5. Start doing some breathing to open up your chest and lungs. Breathe in and hold for 3 seconds and exhale, repeat that 3 times.

6. Sit still a moment and empty your mind of any thoughts that you don't want so you can be ready to experience a clearing or meditative conversation with yourself. Allow a few minutes for this to happen.

7. Try to stay awake and imagine yourself covered in an orb of white protective light that will help you connect to the Angels. You can also hold a clear quartz crystal in your left hand to amplify messages from the Angelic Realm.

8. For example, set your intention that you would like to talk to:

   - **Archangel Michael** for protection and strength or
   - **Archangel Raphael** for healing or for an answer to a specific question

9. Now visualise yourself climbing up 8 stairs and at the top you are greeted by one of the Archangels you have asked to connect with.

10. Now you can ask the Archangel the question you have for them or ask for guidance and wait patiently for an answer.

It may take you a few times to feel you are connected, that is fine as you are learning to use a new muscle. You can also write down the message in a journal, either the same one you keep for your dreams or a new one for Angels.

Calling an Angel

We all have a Guardian Angel we can call on for assistance. Ask them to help you with everything you do.
Jo Brothers

Angels are caring, loving spiritual helpers that can help you to connect with the Celestial Worlds. It has been said that the Universe is the handwriting of Angels. You have a personal Guardian Angel, and can call on the Angels for assistance and invite them into your life.

- **Ariel** guardian of animals and nature, healing, love and creative energy.
- **Chamuel** guardian of unconditional love, emotional healing, romantic love and Soulmates.
- **Gabriel** guardian of communication, transformation, change and emotion.
- **Daniel** guardian of spiritual guidance, your Soul's life purpose, intuition, strength, willpower and courage.
- **Jophiel** guardian of joy, creativity, liberation and education.
- **Michael** guardian of protection, strength, empowerment and compassion.
- **Raguel** guardian of justice and harmony.
- **Raphael** guardian of healing, science, learning/knowledge and oneness.
- **Raziel** guardian allowing access to the secrets of the Universe and your Soul.

- **Uriel** guardian of unconditional love, overcoming difficult challenges and achieving balance.
- **Zadkiel** guardian of compassion, love and forgiveness.

Spiritual Me at Work

You need to feel happy while you are at work. You will spend most of your waking time there so ensure it is working for you, your talents, your goals and your mental, emotional and physical well-being.

Jo Brothers

Many of you work with hundreds or thousands of colleagues whether you work in an office, store, restaurant, hotel, airport, school, university, hospital, factory, mechanical environment or any other place of work.

Some of you are in offices with large open plan seating where you can find yourself in the middle of upward of forty people who all have different energy, different ways of expressing their stress, fear and frustration. Equally some of you may be dealing with customers who are also like this and are challenging to communicate with and could be energetically out of balance.

On the other side there are always good people everywhere who bring lighter energy and are balanced, happy, fun, and are good friends who you can laugh with and work in harmony together. Some jobs require you to wear a uniform or to dress formally and you may feel you have to be a 'different' person at work than when you are at home. Of course you need to be professional and do your job to the best of your ability. However you need to stay true to yourself, being your authentic self, **as** that is the essence of what will help you enjoy life and 'the job' 8 hours a day.

So let us look at some coping techniques to help you. When working with people who do not manage their personal energy well, their stress, fear and heavy energy affects everyone around them. If you are reading this book, you will be sensitive to energy and environments.

Techniques to help the stressed and fearful people around You

- Smiling and being kind to these people can go a long way to helping calm them down.
- Call in the Angels (e.g. Archangel Michael) and ask him to work with this person to calm the situation down.

Techniques to Stay Upbeat and Happy at Work

- You can set this intention and mantra, **"I am safe, and I am capable of anything and everything I imagine"**.
- You can ask Archangel Michael to clothe you in a protective blue light.
- If possible, try listening to your favourite music. Music can realign and calm you or help you to cancel out the noise/energy around you.
- Develop friendships with some of your colleagues, as laughter and happiness is really the best way to create good energy and this will attract Angels to the area.
- If possible go for a walk during a break or at lunch time to move away and break out of the energy. You will return energised and ready to start anew.
- If possible create a haven for yourself at your desk, station or in a locker. Develop a space that brings your personality to that environment, whether it is a stress ball, a pink sparkling stapler, perfume or photos of you, your loved ones, family, children and friends, to anchor yourself to your Spiritual Me and the strong unique Soul that you are.

Some of us are more sensitive to energies around us, so if you feel you have tapped into energy that is not yours, then a swim in the ocean or a pool can cleanse those feelings. Next best option would be a bath or shower. Set your intention to cleanse yourself of all energies that are not your own. For example, **"As I enter the water I release all negative energy from my body."**

Injection of Light

Positivity is the antidote for any negative thought. May your consciousness dwell in positive energy.

Jo Brothers

Here is a great collection of mantras, thoughts and statements that can help you reach internal peace when you are feeling fearful, aggrieved or conflicted. Once the Spiritual Butler Consciousness has located an issue you can now check the list below to see if any of these antidotes can help you.

Check for any recurring negative thoughts you are having and breathe in the positive energy as you read the 'antidote'. I have used these to help me when I have needed to reboot my consciousness and to be honest sometimes I did not feel like reading them, however I always went back to them as I appreciate them and they do work. They help get your positive vibes back in control of the steering wheel of your mind. Tip from me, the more you appreciate all the blessings you have in your life, the quicker you will receive more blessings.

Remember

You are loved and needed, so be you and share your unique gift with the World.

Negative Thought #1
For every job, relationship or new beginning that did not work out.
Antidote #1
I have learnt something from this experience and the best is yet to come.

Negative Thought #2
Feeling tired, lethargic, lazy or unenthused to start a project.
Antidote #2
My future depends on what I do now.

Negative Thought #3
Feeling fearful.
Antidote #3
I have absolute certainty that I am protected and safe, so I move forward with confidence.

Negative Thought #4
It is not the right time to start my project or tomorrow I will start.
Antidote #4
Do not wait, the time will never be just right, so I must start now.

Negative Thought #5
How will I ever achieve my goals?
Antidote #5
I have the power to manifest all my dreams with love.

Negative Thought #6
I do not know if my dreams and goals are worth bringing to life?
Antidote #6
My unique ideas and energy are what the World needs, so I manifest them now.

Negative Thought #7
My life is not what I want it to be.
Antidote #7
I am on the road to good things, so I keep going until I like what I see.

Negative Thought #8
I feel stuck in my life.
Antidote #8
All blockages are illusion, so I will move forward and create the life I want.

Negative Thought #9
Why has this happened to me - seriously?
Antidote #9
Everything happens for me to grow.

Negative Thought #10
I am too old, too tall, too skinny, too fat, too pretty, too ugly...
Antidote #10
The Universe responds to energy, so I emit positive energy.

Negative Thought #11
I feel guilty doing something for me when I know I have so much to do at home.
Antidote #11
Taking responsibility means looking after 'me', as well as everyone else.

Negative Thought #12
I feel stressed!!!
Antidote #12
Breathe! Meditate! Go for a walk. Fuel your Soul by listening to soothing music.

Negative Thought #13
This person really annoys me - Argh!!!
Antidote #13
Everyone I meet has a lesson for me, so I see what I need to learn. Breathe!

Negative Thought #14
I feel alone.
Antidote #14
I am never alone! Angels watch over you, so call on them to help you. Archangel Michael for protection or Archangel Raphael for healing.

Negative Thought #15
I do not like my life.
Antidote #15
Every day is an opportunity to start again and rewrite my story.

Negative Thought #16
People around me are so draining!!!
Antidote #16
Limit your time around these people and check-in with yourself. What frequency do I transmit? Is it Love, Joy or what?

You can make up your own antidotes and write them up in the Notes section at the end of this book.

Words have Power

I am bold, I make, do and ignite, I am present in the Now and I support others in their success.
Jo Brothers

Take time every week to honour your own Soul/spirit and acknowledge the great gifts you have within you that you can share with others.

You can help the World and connect by saying out loud what resonates with you:

- I am Consciousness
- I Create
- I Share
- I am present and in the Now
- I Trust
- I am Proactive
- I am Consistent
- I have Perfect Health and Wellbeing
- I am Creative
- I am a Goddess
- I have Harmony
- I am Perfect as I Evolve
- I am Sensitive
- I Share my Blessings

- I Give and Receive Love
- I have Loving Power
- I am Confident
- I am Excited
- I am Brave
- I am Forgiving
- I Inspire Others
- I am Happy and Share Happiness
- I Respect Everyone
- Were all ONE
- I am LIGHT
- Were all LIGHT
- I have Faith
- Feminine Energy
- Masculine Energy
- I Make, Do and Ignite
- I am Respectful
- I Visualise to Create
- I am Strong
- I am at Peace with Myself
- I have Absolute Certainty
- I am Passionate
- I am Bold

- I am Aware
- I am Magnificent
- I am Collaborative
- I Support others to their Success

You can make up your own words of power and write them up in the Notes section at the end of this book.

Mercury in Retrograde

Mercury in Retrograde can be seen as a time when things are going 'topsy-turvy', but it is a great time to reflect and 'Let Go' of anything that is no longer serving you.
Jo Brothers

Mercury in Retrograde is a phase that happens three times a year for three and a half weeks when the planet Mercury (that rules communication) goes into a resting or sleeping state. Mercury in Retrograde will occur four times in 2016.

Mercury in Retrograde starts:

- January 5th, 2016
- April 28th, 2016
- August 30th, 2016
- December 19th, 2016

Mercury in Retrograde ends:

- January 25th, 2016
- May 22nd, 2016
- September 22nd, 2016
- January 8th, 2016

What areas of your life are impacted by Mercury in Retrograde?

Mail, News, Communication, Agreements, Documents,

Travel, Computers, IT, Cars and Mechanical issues.

So when Mercury is in Retrograde be alert:

- Delays
- Miscommunication
- Do not make any important decisions (if possible)
- Do not sign any documents (if possible)
- Do not launch or start anything new during this time
- Pay attention to details
- Feelings of confusion and being in limbo
- There are often issues with cars, computers not working, travel glitches and delays

Message in a Book

There are messages all around us. All we have to do is open a book.

Jo Brothers

I love this tool and have been using it from a young age for fun and as I grew older for wisdom and guidance. It is an old practice that dates back hundreds of years.

How to get a message in a book

- You have a question that you ask in your mind or out loud.

- You can also invite Archangel Michael to help you find the right book/ebook to receive your message.

- Find a book or ebook.

- Open the book at any random page and read what is inside.

- There will be a message for you there and it usually makes sense if not for the question you asked, it will make sense for something else you have on your mind.

Take Action

Small actions every day build into huge success over time. Appreciate yourself for all the good you do every day.
                                                            Jo Brothers

Every day thank the Universe, Creator or God for all the blessings you already have in your life. Then ask for more help, more LIGHT and more blessings. Make your own appreciation/gratitude list and say, think or read them as often as you can each day. Spend some time saying, reading and thinking positive creating words like these each day.

3 Steps on Taking Action

1. Connect - You Are The Secret - Remember to connect to the LIGHT at all times. You can ask the Universe, Creator or God for help every day; in fact it is more desirable to ask for help every day rather than just calling-in when chaos strikes. Ask to be filled with LIGHT and infinite blessings, try it, what have you got to lose?

2. Channel - Take Action - To channel is to connect to your higher awareness and to receive a message. Find yourself a quiet space, get a pen and paper, sit down and feel yourself relax. Select the question you wish to channel, sit a moment, and start repeating the question in your mind and write down what comes to your mind.

3. Create - Take Action - Create Positive Angels. You create positive Angels by sharing, especially when it is difficult. For example, when you are short of time and had planned to do something for yourself but a friend or family member needs help, you then help them. Sharing can be information, time, a meal, helping someone move house, caring, being empathetic with others and offering to volunteer. You can also donate to support a cause your family or friend are fundraising for or pay it forward and donate to a stranger.

Goddess Power

The divine feminine is within all of us, whether you are female or male, as it is the energy of manifesting, creating life, beginnings and renewal.

__Jo Brothers__

Return of the Goddess Mantra

Calling in the Mother energy of mankind to restore humanity to feminine vibration of mind.

All that is to be will now come forth from the gateways of South, East, West and North.

All feminine energies return to the Earth Plane to shine, love, light and passion and feminine vibration of mind.

Any female being suppressed or bullied feel your strength return.

Help shape a kinder, loving, peaceful humanity - this we all must learn.

All blockages dissolve into nothing, triumph is ours.

We are here to help mankind, as God has allowed.

Return of the Goddess, the time is NOW!

Total global feminine integration to all, to all who allow!

Faith has kept us whole, go in peace today.

The light has won! And always will, come what may!

Mother, Mother, Mother

__Jo Brothers 2006__

I wrote this mantra, power prayer, called Return of the Goddess in 2006. It was published on a website of mine and in a few other places, however it has remained largely concealed up until now. I feel now is the perfect time to share it in this book for you to read and connect to the Feminine Energy. Often a lot of what you read about the Creator, God, and Buddha is Masculine Energy.

However, there is a Feminine Energy that walks alongside and is part of the duality of life, it is the Feminine Energy that creates, manifests, gives birth, nurtures, nourishes and transforms. As women and men we should feel open to include and accept a Feminine aspect of Spirituality and Energy, as the World is in need of a balance of Feminine Energy at this time on Earth.

Code

Wherever you go and whatever you do, you are You!
Jo Brothers

Your code is the natural style you operate in, in both your working and social environments. Decide which of these codes you are and remember they are equally important, with one being more dominate at any given time.

What is the code you live by and are you a Thinker, Leader, Doer, Campaigner or Organiser?

Thinker is a person that is a fast thinker, interprets ideas quickly and can apply them to different concepts. Thinks of big ideas but needs support to make things happen.

Leader is a person that is able to easily develop relationships and connect with people. Is able to energise and have people passionately following them in any business or organisation and is loyal and has a loyal team.

Doer is a person that is supportive, loves being part of something, a company, a project or a charity event and adds value. They are happy to follow plans and do set tasks to move a project or event forward.

Campaigner is a person that is a team player, loves being part of something and adds value by promoting and networking to take the news of what is happening out into the wider community and the World.

Organiser is a person that is organised, loves the detail, plans, charts, timekeeping and bookkeeping. Is able to develop strategies and clearly communicate these to others.

Great so now that you know your code, you can begin to connect with it and use it in both your working and social environments.

Super Power

We are all super beyond our dreams and we all have powers. So connect to yours and use it to help yourself and others every day.

Jo Brothers

You will have Super Powers, with one that is the more dominant when dealing with yourself, loved ones, friends, colleague and the World.

Which of these Super Powers do you feel you have?

Generosity, you are generous with your time and are always there for people. The energy of generosity flows as your natural state is to help others, supporting them with time or money. Whether it is being supportive by listening to a loved one, friend or colleague at a time when they need it.

Patience, you are able to see the big picture of your life and move forward step by step knowing you will reach and achieve all of your dreams and goals. In your daily life this helps you to appreciate the little things and as you radiate an inner peace you influence everyone around you. People seek you out for advice.

Humility/Humble, you are most likely successful, popular and very humble with it. You make time for everyone and do not expect any special treatment. In fact you could actually be shy and prefer to spend your personal time with close family, friends and loved ones.

Kindness, you are kind, and emanate a wonderful happy joyful energy. People seek you out for assistance and you help them. Since like attracts like, you usually have like-minded friends who behave in a similar way to you. Your presence encourages others to behave the same way and kindness radiates out into the World from you and your circle of friends and family.

Balance, you have a busy life, at home, at work, hobbies and children and somehow you can fit more in than most people. You are masterful at managing your time and prioritising what to do when and how much time to spend on activities at home and at work. People who see you do not know how you manage it as you always appear calm and carefree.

Dedication, you take on large or long-term projects and see them through to success and completion. Whether it is a challenge at work, a volunteer project or a sports goal you are focused and determined. Some people may not understand your laser like focus' however on completion of your project they will see the magnitude of your accomplishment.

Creative, you are a natural problem solver, you do not like rules and you create new ways of doing things. Many creatives are innovators, designers and visionaries. More than likely some of your ideas are visionary and that can scare some people who do not like change. That does not bother you, as you know what you are doing and the creative energy flows through you at work and at home.

Spiritual Me Intention Compass

We are all made up of many things and when we take the time to review, we see the big picture of our skills and potential.
Jo Brothers

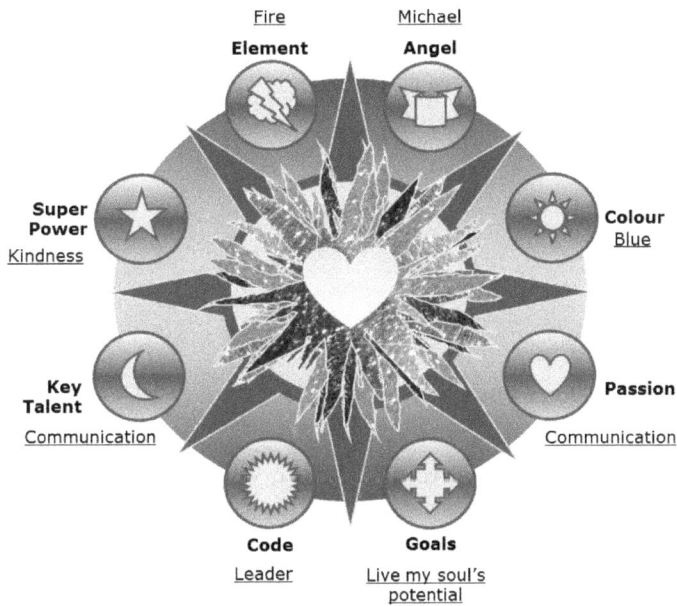

Example of a Spiritual Me Intention Compass

Here is a quick exercise for you to create your very own Spiritual Me Intention Compass.

1. Who is your personal Angel?

Which Angel did you connect to?

---

2. What is your favourite Colour?

According to the 7 chakra colours.

---

3. What is your Passion?

---

4. What are your ultimate Goals in life?

_____
_____
_____

5. What is your Code?

Are you a Thinker, Leader, Doer, Campaigner or Organiser?

_____
_____
_____

6. What is your Key Talent?

For example, Communication

_____
_____
_____

7. What is your Super Power?

Are you a Generous, Patient, Humble, Kind, Balanced or Dedicated?

8. What is your Element?

Do you resonate best near earth, water, air or fire?

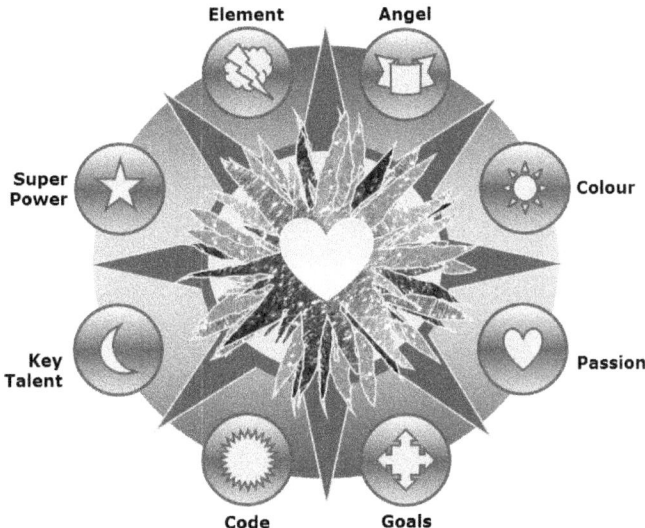

Your Spiritual Me Intention Compass

Love Your Body

You truly are perfect exactly as you are. Love yourself and Love your body.
                                                                    Jo Brothers

We are all different, you need to find what is right for you and it could be all or none of the following. Personally I use all of these healing methods and find that they add to my wellbeing, happiness, vitality and health.

Massage, yes absolutely. If you can get a massage go for it! Whether it is a partner, friend, professional masseuse, masseur, or massage therapist that gives you a relaxing massage. It will release trapped energy in your muscles, de-stressing you and allowing you to relax, feeling recharged and energised. A Reflexology massage is great as it works on the pressure points in your feet and along your spine (Chakra's), restoring energy and releasing blockages.

Chiropractor, again yes absolutely. I have found having regular chiropractic care has helped me in mind, body and Soul. Chiropractors most often treat the neuromusculoskeletal including pain in the back, neck, joints, arms, legs, ankles and knees.

Acupuncture has its origins in traditional Chinese medicine and is great to relieve a wide range of pain and stress related body issues when administered by a trained practitioner.

Exercise is important for your wellbeing mind, body and Soul. Keep moving, walking, stretching, going to the gym, paddling in a kayak, cycling, doing Yoga or Pilates, whatever resonates with you. It is said that we are more inclined to make healthier food choices if we have exercised.

Spiritual Growth

Lasting inner happiness and harmony comes from nurturing your mind, body and Soul/spirit.

Jo Brothers

It is most important that you have a solid connection to who you are, and to knowing that you are capable of anything you visualise or imagine and that you have no idea of the awesomeness of your potential.

Yes, it is good to set goals and achieve them. However the only person you should be comparing yourself to, is you and who you were last year. Have you changed? Have you grown?

Remember growth happens when you are outside of your comfort zone.

Competing with a colleague at work or a friend is counter-productive to your energy and is a waste of time. The only person you need to compete with is yourself, to become the best version of yourself. If you take a look at me waiting to complete this book, I read my work from 2007 and felt I was reading notes from a younger sister, not myself. So, great I can see I have personally grown and have learnt a lot and am more my real me, more authentic.

Let us define compete - to practice again and again, trying your hardest to improve each time. Professional athletes will always seek out their coaches after finishing a race, run, swim or game and ask questions like, **"Where do you think I went wrong?"** or **"What could I have done better?"**, as they know that these are the areas they need to work on. So, it is a good idea to review your past week at a time that suits you in the weekend, to see if you wish you could have done a few things differently.

A Final Word

Thank You for reading this book. I truly hope it helps You connect to your potential and miracles flowing in your life.
                                                              Jo Brothers

You are in total control of your life. You have the power to change every aspect of your life at any time.

You do not need to live with regrets as every day you have the opportunity to seize the day and create your destiny, your legacy.

What defines you in the end is being true to you. Living as your authentic real self and in doing so, you inspire others to do the same.

Remember to love large, share often, be united with your community with love in your heart, treat everyone as you would like to be treated and live a joyful, purposeful magnificent life.

Make a difference in the World! I know you can!

You are wonderful just the way you are and you have infinite potential.

 Jo

xox

PS. Feel free to message me on www.spiritualme101.com or www.facebook.com/spiritualme101 to say Hi or to share your journey.

Notes

May messages of inspiration, passion and joy fill these pages.
Jo Brothers

www.ingramcontent.com/pod-product-compliance
Lightning Source LLC
Chambersburg PA
CBHW050843160426
43192CB00011B/2128